Thanksgiving for the Gift of a Child

A Commentary on the
Common Worship Service

Trevor Lloyd

Archdeacon of Barnstaple and a
Consultant to the Liturgical Commission

GROVE BOOKS LIMITED

RIDLEY HALL RD CAMBRIDGE CB3 9HU

Contents

Note

Page numbers refer to the full edition of *Common Worship: Pastoral Services* (Church House Publishing, November 2000). The author is grateful for permission to use some material from this book, which is © The Archbishops' Council of the Church of England, 2000.

The author is also grateful to Margaret Baxter and Anne Hollinghurst for their stories in Chapter 5, to his former colleague Anne Salisbury who was the original drafter of 'You can't leave the vicar holding this baby' quoted in the same chapter, and to Mark Earey for detailed suggestions on the contents and original draft of the booklet.

The Cover Illustration is by Peter Ashton

First Impression August 2001
ISSN 0144-1728
ISBN 1 85174 474 6

1

Occasion and Opportunity

Family Snaps 1

It is Sunday afternoon. The church is full of people, noisy with young families, gurgling babies and runaround toddlers. Some seem very much at home; some families know each other; others look a bit apprehensive. A group of musicians play softly in the background. At the door, some church members are welcoming people—they are part of the young families pastoral team. Two of them are involved in leading some of the five playgroups and parents and toddlers groups the church runs on weekdays. So that is why some of the families know each other. It is all part of a strategy of meeting the needs, both practical and spiritual, of the families in the local community.

This service only happens four or five times a year, so regular church members know when it is (many of them are involved in providing cakes and sandwiches for the tea which follows), and invite their friends. It is something the whole church has been involved in since the young families team produced a leaflet—'You can't leave the vicar holding this baby!' (see chapter 5).

Family Snaps 2

It is Saturday afternoon and Alistair and Clare have invited a dozen of their close friends and family round to a party to celebrate the formal arrival of their newly-adopted son, Joseph. After seemingly endless months of interviews and a trial placement, the bits of paper have been signed and there seems a lot to celebrate. One of their friends is the curate from the local church, who suggested using the Thanksgiving Service as part of the celebrations, so she leads a very informal time of worship, with Alistair and Clare's older children taking part and other friends praying.

Family Snaps 3

It is Sunday morning and the large congregation at St Oswald's-in-the-Suburbs wakes up as Tim and Alison's baby cries into the microphone Tim is wearing. It is just after the sermon and the vicar is asking them some informal questions about their specific intention to bring the child up within the faith, which gives them both an opportunity for testimony. Tim and Alison, like some other families in the church, come from a Baptist background and would really have liked an 'infant dedication' service, but they are very happy with this angle on the Thanksgiving Service, and have

3

invited a good number of their friends and some non-Christian relatives along for the occasion. One of their friends later leads the prayers.

Family Snaps 4
It is Sunday morning and the Family Service in the village church. Nearly everyone knows Mike and Jane's new baby arrived ten days ago, and they are here in church for the first time since Jasmin arrived. No one is surprised when the vicar, after a brief informal introduction, invites Mike, Jane and the baby to the front, and asks 'do you receive Jasmin as a gift from God?' This is followed by the prayer of blessing, the giving of the gospel (by the churchwarden) and some more prayers for the family, before the rest of the Family Service continues.

Family Snaps 5
It is Monday morning, and Fiona is recovering in a side ward at the hospital after a gruesomely long and complicated labour in which she nearly lost the baby. Her husband James has been by her side most of the night, and their very precious Jeremy, looking a bit battered, is there in an incubator. They are regular church-goers but had decided that they did not want their baby baptized immediately because they thought they should wait until he was old enough to take part in the decision. Caroline, their vicar, arrives and suggests the Thanksgiving Service as the most appropriate thing to do, there and then. The words 'We thank you for all whose support and skill surround and sustain the beginning of life' take on a special poignancy, and she uses the special prayer for use after a difficult birth: 'Loving Father, you have turned pain into joy…'

These five snapshots of the Thanksgiving Service in use show some of the occasions for which it was designed. These are helpfully outlined in the Note at the beginning of the service:

This service is provided for a number of different occasions:
- the private celebration of a birth or adoption, at home or in church with only family and close friends present;
- the public celebration of the birth or adoption of a number of children, perhaps in church on a Sunday afternoon;
- the public celebration of the birth or adoption or a number of children as part of a main Sunday act of worship.

It is designed to meet the needs of:
- parents who see this as a preliminary to Baptism;
- parents who do not wish their children to be baptized immediately;

4

- others, who do not ask for Baptism, but who recognize that something has happened for which they wish to give thanks to God.

So this is different from the *Book of Common Prayer* service of The Thanksgiving of Women after Childbirth, commonly called The Churching of Women. That service is focussed on the woman and her deliverance 'from the great pain and peril of childbirth.' There is no mention of the baby, who may not have survived and in any case need not be in church; nor is there any mention of a husband, apart from the allusion in the psalm: 'Happy is the man who has his quiver full of them.' The service had an ancient origin, being mentioned in a letter from St Augustine to Gregory the Great around 601, but had lost the mediaeval overtones of purification. These linger in the 'Churching' bit of the title, and in the 1549 closing rubric about offerings: 'The woman that is purified, must offer her Chrism...' By 1552 it was purely thanksgiving.

The *Common Worship* service focuses not on the woman, but on the child. In theory at least the mother might have died in childbirth, but there could still be a thanksgiving for the arrival of the child. Note 2 makes it clear that there might only be one parent present. And the child might have arrived not by birth but by adoption. The emphasis is on the child as part of the family, with prayers for mother, father and other children, even for grandparents and other relatives.

There are changes, too, from the *Alternative Service Book*. The ASB had two separate services, Thanksgiving for the Birth of a Child, and Thanksgiving after Adoption, and saw the church as the normal place for the services to be used. *Common Worship* has one very flexible service which can be used at home, in hospital or at church. It does not start with the mediaeval question, 'How can we encourage and allow this woman back into our holy building?' but with the more homely and contemporary question, 'Tell us how you feel about the arrival of this child, and we will see if we can express that in prayer and thanksgiving.'

One further point to note which follows naturally from the fact that this service is not about getting back into church, but an opportunity to give thanks in other locations too, is that there is no restriction about who may take this service. The Revision Committee report (GS1298Y, May 1999) states 'The two final Blessing Prayers have been italicized to make it clear that they can be used by Readers and other Ministers.' This not only increases the scope for lay ministry but enables a family friend or relative to lead such a service in the home.

2
Stages on the Way, Blessing and Friends

The fundamental conceptual differences between this service and that in the ASB can be seen when the service is put back into the context in which it was first drafted. Michael Vasey, tutor in liturgy at Cranmer Hall, Durham, for 23 years, died in June 1998 having just completed work on *Rites on the Way: Work in Progress* (General Synod Miscellaneous Paper 530, July 1998). This draft set of prayers and forms of service was something the Liturgical Commission had been working on, with Michael as the chief drafter, to provide the portfolio of rites and prayers surrounding baptism and confirmation, called for by the earlier report *On the Way* (Church House Publishing, 1995). In the earlier drafts *Thanksgiving and Blessing of a Child* had been part of this package, but was published as a separate draft for Synod (GS1298, May 1998), simply because it was seen as an alternative to the BCP service and therefore subject to the approval—and processes—of the General Synod.

On the Way had argued that 'sacramental rites should not be seen as isolated transactions but rather should be integrated with the social and spiritual processes which they represent.' This contextualization was not simply a matter of setting down a number of stages on the road to baptism, but a surrounding of the whole journey, and a number of possible by-paths and diversions, with prayer and spiritual activity. And this was to be based, not just on what the church might see as the stages and requirements on the way to baptism, but on a deep understanding of, and identification with, the human and social longings and aspirations, hopes and fears, pains and joys which accompany them. Michael's Jewish and African background, as well as his experience of pain and vulnerability, enabled him to understand, compile and write material in this area with a skill which others on the Commission found it hard to emulate, so that this work is still incomplete three years after his death. He drafted part of an introduction to this section of the book:

> The reception of a child into the human community is an important moment. It is appropriate both for the child, for the parents and for the community that it should be marked in significant ways. The creation of a new human being within the relationship of two people is a wonder of creation. However, baptism is not a birth rite but the application to the individual of the life-changing coming of Jesus Christ into the world. Baptism is not simply a beginning, it is a reality into which we grow all our lives. The forms of service that follow are not replacements for baptism; they are intended to enable families to bring the mystery of their

life into the presence of God and to enable them, where they so wish, to grow into the new reality that God has made known to us in Jesus Christ and declares to us in the sacrament of baptism.

So we find in that collection forms for blessing a pregnant woman and a couple expecting a child, prayers for conception (which were said to have worked!), prayers for use with a mother after the birth of a child, for a sick mother, for a child born with special needs, for use after a miscarriage and after a stillbirth. The new Thanksgiving Service sits firmly in this context, and is to be seen, not in isolation but as part of a staged process. 'Prayers after Birth,' Michael wrote, 'attempts to build on recent studies that suggest that the old Churching of Women fulfilled an important social role in supporting women in the ambiguities of motherhood...the rite aims at simplicity and gives no instruction about the minister.' In the draft, the Thanksgiving Service comes after this and has a different focus, as we have already seen.

If the Thanksgiving Service is clearly removed from Churching, so it also stands at some distance from Baptism. The themes in the readings and phrases of the liturgy in the Baptism services are those of the crucifixion and resurrection; in the Thanksgiving Service they are those of creation and incarnation: this is where the thanksgiving is grounded. They come at radically different points in the journey.

But, with this fundamental difference clear, Michael could then argue for the service to include godparents, naming and blessing, three elements deliberately excluded from the ASB service.

I still think that it is a mistake to focus on making the service as different as possible from baptism rather than asking what ought to belong to a service of thanksgiving and prayer. This service is structured around the concept of prayer rather than interrogation.

Naming and Blessing

The report of the Ely Commission on *Christian Initiation* published in June 1971, which recommended that the Liturgical Commission should produce a new Service of Thanksgiving for the birth of a child for general use throughout the church, sought to distinguish the new service from Baptism. 'The rite of entry into the Christian society is Baptism and...there can be no other.' (p 36). Blessing is to be allowed: 'Blessing, as applied to infants, is primarily thanksgiving; persons are blessed by thanking God for them. This has nothing to do with Baptism.' But naming is not:

Naming should not be associated with blessing. As a civil action, naming is done by the parents and the registrar. As a liturgical action, naming is the setting of God's seal on the personal, 'civil' name...At Baptism the personal name of the individual is brought into relation with the three-fold Name of God into which he [sic] is baptized...Forenames become Christian names. Naming is essentially a baptismal act, and has no place in a Service of Thanksgiving.

The Doctrine Commission's report *Baptism Thanksgiving and Blessing*, produced in the same year, took the view that blessing the child was acceptable, so long as it was not in the form 'N, I bless thee in the name of the Father...' The services in ASB did not include any explicit blessing of the child. *Thanksgiving for the Gift of a Child* has followed the position of the earlier Doctrine Commission report while taking care not to give the blessing a 'solemn' or formulaic character that could be confused with baptism.

One of the problems over naming the child is that since the middle ages there has been a popular concept that children receive their name at baptism. This led to the fear that any emphasis on the name of the child at Thanksgiving might lead to a confusion of this service with baptism. The idea that a person receives his or her name at baptism may be seriously misleading if it is linked with the idea that the human and Christian community are co-terminous and thus fails to see God as committed to, and active in, the wider human community. In modern society it is clear to people that children receive their name before baptism. The Liturgical Commission in 1998 responded favourably to the inclusion of the name, agreeing with the argument that the direct link between baptism and naming is a surprisingly late development in Western baptismal liturgy, and that the recovery of adult baptism makes it desirable to break this link. The *Common Worship* service is framed on the assumption that the given name of a child can be celebrated as a sign of the uniqueness of the child and of God's commitment to the child in love. Establishing that the child is known by God before baptism and separating the celebration of the name from baptism should help the true meaning of baptism to stand out.

The ASB has neither blessing nor naming. The *Common Worship* service both asks a parent or supporting friend the name of the child, and asks for God's blessing on the child:

The minister may say for each child:
What name have you given this child?
....As Jesus took children in his arms and blessed them,
so now we ask God's blessing on N.

These carefully constructed texts in fact neither name nor bless, as actions within the service. The parents are asked what name they have already given the child at the register office (in other words, this is not the moment at which the champagne bottle is broken open—'I name this child...'), and the prayer for blessing is not performative (as after a sneeze) but precatory: 'surround *him/her* with your blessing.'

Supporting Friends

Another step towards similarity with baptism which makes sense in our current cultural climate is the provision for 'supporting friends' who stand with the parents at the thanksgiving, may present the child to the minister, and may speak informally at that point in the service. At an early stage of the drafting there was also provision for godparents, on the grounds that if the child is soon to be baptized and the godparents have already been asked, it makes more sense to include them here, but—as the Doctrine Commission report had said two decades earlier—it was thought that to mention them might be confusing. But there is no reason why they should not be among the 'supporting friends,' and this is one of the pastoral strengths of the service. Sometimes non-church-going parents have invited people to be godparents before realizing that it may not be appropriate to proceed immediately to the baptism of their child. In addition on occasion people choose as godparents those who have supported them as they have prepared for the arrival of their child rather than those who could exercise a supporting role in the future. The small (and optional) liturgical role for 'supporting friends' may help in these situations, and it is clearly distinguished from the later role of godparents which remains firmly linked to baptism.

There can be any number of 'supporting friends' (and unlike godparents, they do not need to be baptized, or confirmed or practising Christians). They could be agnostics or Muslims. Note 4 explains that their commitment is to the child and the family. Nowhere in the service do they express any commitment to the church or the Christian faith. There is also provision for the wider circle of family and friends to commit themselves to help and support the family. The ASB service does not envisage the presence of godparents or supporting friends, and does not allow for any commitment—of any sort—to be expressed.

Apart from these three theologically-motivated differences from the ASB service there are others, such as the provision of a Pastoral Introduction, a wider selection of Bible Readings, a larger selection of prayers which engage with different situations, and making the giving of a Gospel no longer optional but a central part of the service. Nor is there a substantial prayer for the parents to recite together, as in section 2 of the ASB service. Michael Vasey wrote about the possible embarrassment of parents with reading difficulties, and the danger of putting words into their mouths: 'The ASB's prayer feels manipulative. ("If you want a sweet, you must say sorry to Grandma nicely").'

9

3
Expectations and Ecclesiology

The Introduction to the *Common Worship: Pastoral Services* volume sees the Thanksgiving service as one of the stages on the road, part of the journey towards baptism. 'It is at such key moments in people's lives that they are often prompted to ask serious questions and even to turn to God. Here there is also provision for those who accompany others on the journey, as words are given for supporting friends, standing alongside the parents welcoming a new member of the family' (*Common Worship: Pastoral Services*, 2000, p 5).

All of these stages on the road mark crisis points in life, at which people have good reason to reflect, wonder, fear, rejoice, and ask questions about the meaning of life and the universe. Willimon puts succinctly what is happening, and what the needs are, in any rite of passage as people make the transition from one stage of life to the next.

> From anthropology and comparative religion came the image of a ritual as a rite of passage. Rites of passage are ritualized journeys across life's most difficult boundaries. They give meaning to the changes in status or role of persons, they re-establish equilibrium in persons and communities after the crisis of change, and they serve the educational function of transmitting to future generations what the community believes to be the meaning of that change. (Willimon, W, *Worship as Pastoral Care*, Abingdon Nashville, 1979, p 102)

The Pastoral Introduction to the service itself captures some of this:

> The birth or adoption of a child is a cause for celebration. Many people are overcome by a sense of awe at the creation of new life and want to express their thanks to God. This service provides an opportunity for parents and families to give thanks for the birth or adoption of a child and to pray for family life.

And it encourages people to make the most of this opportunity:

> If you are interested in exploring the Christian faith, or finding out more about preparation for Baptism, ask the minister taking this service.

So for some people the Thanksgiving service will clearly have many of the elements and expectations of a rite of passage, providing that necessary ritualization of the change in status from being childless to being parents, publicly welcoming and integrating a new arrival into the community, and passing on some of what they think to be the meaning of that change. Changes at different stages in life are often best marked by thanksgiving—giving thanks to God for the event and for what has led up to it. Even at death enough space needs to be given to thanksgiving for the life of the one who has died. The Thanksgiving service majors on this element:

We are here today to give thanks for these children...

There is thanksgiving for the process which has led to this point:

We thank you for all whose support and skill
Surround and sustain the beginning of life.

There is thanksgiving for this particular named individual and thanksgiving for this particular family and his or her arrival into it. There is the possibility of thanksgiving for grandparents, and even when a child with special needs has been entrusted to the family.

Recognition and Value

In human terms, the service meets the need of an occasion to express recognition and value. The occasion recognizes what has happened (the new arrival), recognizes the child by name, values them in their humanity with a separate name, and values the family into which they have come. The very gathering itself, whether at home or in church, is an expression of that complicated network of relationships within which, from now on, they will find their place. Providing a service like this should at the very least be seen as a contribution by the church to the health of society, enabling the open recognition of complex but supportive relationships. But there is more than that. In spiritual, God-fearing terms, this service says that God values this child and this family, that they and their web of relationships are important to him, but that there is also something beyond them, beyond the human, going on. In the mystery of thanksgiving, praying, hearing the Word, and taking part in the symbolic action of blessing, God is at work opening people's minds to himself.

Expectations

Rites of passage are partly about expectations. There is a time of looking forward to the change that is to happen, then coping with the potential trauma of the change itself, and adjusting to what has happened, with new expectations about the future. So the expectations of a family who might come to a

Thanksgiving service are going to vary. Some will not have thought further than a nice afternoon occasion to which they can invite their friends. For some it will be a very human recognition and rejoicing, in front of friends and family, that their child has arrived, and for some of them that public arrival will have some of the Jewish overtones of the Presentation of Christ in the Temple, the arrival into a close-knit faith community which carries with it implications for the future of the world. For others it will be part of a journey towards baptism, either a welcome stage on the road or a process which has to be endured in order to arrive at the baptism service.

And the church itself will have different expectations. How can a human event be transformed into a spiritual one? Is there one clear message, or a number of different messages, coming across at the Thanksgiving service? How can people be encouraged to take the next step on the road, perhaps to enquire about the Christian faith? Or how do you pray and sense the presence of God in a church full of noisy children and babies without simply going into automatic mode and getting through the words of the service? And how can the members of the church be encouraged to use their spiritual imaginations and to pray for this service and take part in the ministry associated with it?

4
Prayers and Notes

There were considerable changes made to this service during the Revision Stage of its progress through the General Synod. Some members of Synod asked for greater clarity as to the occasions on which the service might be used, which led the Revision Committee into an exchange of stories similar to that found in our first chapter here. This led to two major changes: the provision of an opening Note which sets out clearly the different occasions and the different people for which the service is intended; and the re-casting of the text from the singular into the plural. Instead of seeing the major use of the service as a private family occasion at home, the committee put the service primarily into a church setting, and probably therefore with a number of babies and families present.

One other ecclesiological note is the clarity with which Note 1 follows the ASB practice in insisting that a register should be kept and a certificate given to the parents. The 1972 Doctrine Commission report had insisted that there should be no registers and no certificates—that would make it clear that it was not a baptism. The note in the present service comes both from the pragmatic reasoning that if people forget or are in doubt as to what happened, a certificate would ensure that it was not confused with baptism, and also from the reasoning that this service is in fact owned by the church, part of a process which in many cases may end in Christian initiation, and not an informal hole-in-the-corner kind of event.

Introduction

In early drafts, the service began formally with 'The grace...' This was de-formalized in the Revision Committee so that there could be an informal introduction, or liturgical greetings could be used, and some are provided on p 207. The first of these sets the incarnational flavour of the service:

In the name of Jesus,
Who was born to be our Saviour, Christ the Lord,
We welcome you.

This incarnational flavour is seen right at the end of the service, in the reference in Note 5 to 'hymns, songs or carols,' which might stimulate the use of such incarnational material at times other than Christmas.

A suggestion is given for words to introduce the service, but, again, other words may be more appropriate, depending on the occasion. Certainly at an event in someone's home, this might sound a little pompous.

The heading 'Reading(s) and Sermon,' in line with the other Pastoral Services, was inserted at Revision Stage, and the seventeen suggested readings moved to the Supplementary Texts section at the end of the service. At the same time the rubric was changed from 'One of the following readings (or another suitable reading)...' to 'A suitable passage from the Bible is read (see...) to make it quite clear that the intention was to have a Bible Reading, and not some other kind of reading.

While great care has been taken to ensure that the wording of the service makes it equally appropriate for the adoption of a baby or an older child into a family, some may question the phrase in the prayer of blessing 'Heavenly Father, we praise you for *his/her* birth.' This was in fact carefully considered by the Revision Committee, and it was decided that it was quite appropriate to praise God for the birth of any individual—however old—entering a new family. For the same reason the preceding rubric does not echo the opening line of the prayer, 'As Jesus took children in his arms...,' though in an earlier draft it had read 'The minister may take the child in his or her arms, or may lay a hand on the child and invite others to do so.' This was changed to the simple 'The minister may take the child' for the very good reason that the child might be too big to take into the arms, and also that the church should probably not be seen in print inviting others to lay hands on children, though that is probably a good and symbolic thing to do in many cases.

The prayer 'God our Creator' is a general prayer (adapted from the *Book of Alternative Services* of the Anglican Church in Canada by Mark Earey) which can be said for a number of children together, before moving on to the individual question 'for each child' about the name, followed by the individual prayer of blessing as the minister takes each child in turn. Note 3 explains this and allows for the possibility, for example when there are twins, to say the prayer only once for two children. Then when all the children have been prayed for, the whole congregation says 'may they learn to love....'

The next prayer is one for all the parents and families—'May God the Father of all bless these parents.' It originally had '*N* and *N*' instead of 'these parents' and when there are only two or four names to mention it would be good to use the names rather than 'these parents' and the child's or children's names later in the prayer. Note 3 spells this out.

The Blessing

There was some discussion both on the Liturgical Commission and on the Revision Committee as to whether the Aaronic blessing could only be said by a priest. The conclusion was that it was not necessary to designate this blessing exclusively in this way, but it should be put second after 'The love of the Lord Jesus draw you to himself' and that in both blessings 'you' should be italicized to indicate that 'us' could also be used. Both blessings are in the ASB Thanksgiving service.

Additional Prayers

Prayers 1, 2, and 3 are from the ASB Thanksgiving service.

Prayer 5: For the father. This was drafted by a member of the Steering Committee at the request of the Revision Committee.

Prayer 6: Grandparents and other relatives. The basis of this prayer is a prayer slightly adapted from *A Prayer Book for Australia*, p 46:

> We thank you, heavenly Father,
> that you have set us in families,
> with relatives and friends of all ages.
> Help us to respect and learn from one another.
> We ask that, in this family,
> N may see and enjoy many loving relationships,
> through Jesus Christ, who loves us all. **Amen.**

Lines 5 and 6 were felt to be unfortunately open to misinterpretation in the current climate in England, and changing them led to a more wholesale change in the prayer. This is fairly typical of how one province in the Anglican Communion builds on the work of another, adapting it to its own cultural setting.

Prayer 8: After a difficult birth. This prayer was inserted after a Revision Committee discussion about how far this service might be used in place of the Churching of Women especially for women and children who had survived difficult child birth or a traumatic first few days or weeks after the birth.

A prayer for the birth parents of an adopted child was thought to be essential in cases of adoption, and **Prayer 11** was taken from *A Prayer Book for Australia*, with a change in the first line, away from the echo of the Prayer of Humble Access ('your nature is always to have mercy' might be interpreted as dwelling too heavily on their supposed need for God's mercy) to 'rich in goodness and mercy.'

Another, even more radical, adaptation from Australia is **Prayer 12** when a child has special needs. This was redrafted by the Chairman of the Steering Committee and a member of General Synod who had personal experience of this situation, who had written to object to some of the phrases in the Australian prayer such as 'help them to look to you when frustrated or despairing.' What the parents do not need is the implication that the future holds frustration and despair. It was suggested that something more positive might be said about the things such children contribute to the family. Hence:

That *N* may grow up secure in giving and receiving love
And in the enjoyment of your presence
To enrich our lives and the lives of others
In ways beyond our imagining.

5
Policy and Practice

Churches work with different models and theologies of the church, of baptism and its preliminaries, and of their relationship to the community. The *Common Worship* Thanksgiving service is designed to be a tool that can be used whatever the model or theology of the church. But it is always helpful to have some self-understanding about the nature of the local church, and how this service might be used within that understanding. The Church Council, for instance, might discuss:

- Which picture or model of the church suits us best? Are we a community church, reflecting and penetrating the local community, or a gathered assembly of like-minded individuals, an institution conscious of its links with the past and the need to pass on that tradition to the future, a group of people whose main attraction is in our mutual relationships? Do we see ourselves as the crusading, missionary people of God, or the adoring, worshipping bride of Christ, or the interdependent body of Christ, doing his work in the world? What are the differences in the approach to the Thanksgiving service that might emerge from each of these positions?

- Is there a church mission statement, a parish plan, or a five-year set of aims and objectives? How best can the Thanksgiving service be used in line with these aims?

- Who should be responsible for the Thanksgiving service? Should the vicar be left to do it on her own? Should there be a special group set up to encourage its use, plan the services, and follow up those who come? Or is this best left to some existing group, like a young families ministry team, or baptism preparation group?

- How often should these services be held, and at what time of day?

- How can the PCC benefit from the experience of other churches which have been using such a service for some time?

- What teaching and training might be needed for the congregation? What leaflets, cards, orders of service might be needed? Are there good examples from other places which might give us ideas as we produce something specific for our own situation?

It is worth underlining to any PCC that this is not a novel idea. We have already noted that the 1971 Ely Report recommended that the Liturgical Commission compile such a service. In the same year, I was a member of the London Diocesan Baptism Commission, examining the downward spiral of infant baptism figures in the diocese and making recommendations (agreed by the Diocesan Synod) that PCCs should review their practice of Christian initiation, that baptism must be preceded by preparation, and that a Service of Thanksgiving should be available. The one included in the Report came into use nine years ahead of that in the ASB, and included a mandatory giving of a Gospel and a blessing prayer, 'Bless now we pray this child N...' In 1972 Christopher Byworth and John Simpson wrote Grove Booklet 5, *A Service of Thanksgiving and Blessing*, with a service included which was reprinted and used in many churches, again including a mandatory giving of a Gospel but with no blessing and no space for the mention of a name.

There are, then, quite a number of places with many years of experience. Introducing the Revision Committee report to the General Synod in 1999, Margaret Baxter told a story:

> In my part of England there is still a clear folk memory that 'water is important,' so that of those who look to the church to mark the arrival of a child often want 'the proper service, the one with water.' Church people feel the same. The last time our morning service included Thanksgiving for the birth of a child, the older church members around me were mystified. 'Why isn't it baptism?' They were seriously worried about whether or not this child would be entitled to a church marriage or funeral, and maybe they were worried about hellfire as well.
>
> The truth is that Thomas's parents wanted to give thanks yet did not feel able to make the greater commitment of baptism. And while less and less people bring their babies to church for *any* service, those who insist on 'water' are often not seen in church again. Thomas and his mother are quite often with us on a Sunday morning. Clearly we met a need. Thomas may or may not come to baptism later. Perhaps at seven he will ask to be admitted to communion and have to be prepared for Baptism. But for now he and his parents have become part of our church community, with the opportunities that affords to proclaim to them the message of God's love in Jesus.

Anne Hollinghurst, curate at St Saviour, Nottingham, describes what happens in her multi-cultural, multi-faith Urban Priority Area, where the congregation includes inner-city locals who have lived there all their lives, and a large number of young families who have joined the church as students and stayed on in the area:

The previous incumbent had introduced a system whereby any who wanted their child baptized were first offered a 'Thanksgiving' within the main morning service—this applied to both regular church members and those from the local community who approached the church.

There were some in the church who, though committed people of faith, did not want their child baptized, preferring for it to be the child's decision when older. They did want a chance to celebrate, mark and give thanks for the child however, as well as dedicate their child in some way to God. Those in the church who did want a baptism were happy to have the Thanksgiving as a more immediate rite after the birth, with the baptism following a little later as a bigger family occasion for them.

The real value, however, of offering to everyone a Thanksgiving first came when receiving enquiries about baptism from non-church attenders in the local community. Pastorally, it meant that any enquiry could be met with a warm, positive and welcoming response, along the lines of...'how wonderful, you've had a baby and want to in some way give thanks to God and celebrate this...as the church we welcome you and want to celebrate with you...'

As the same system operated for church members as well, this diminished any idea that the newcomer was being treated as a kind of 'second class citizen.' It was explained that after the Thanksgiving, there would then be the opportunity to talk about the meaning of baptism and go on to this if it felt the right thing. In the meantime, the chance had been created to build up a relationship, give the family a really good occasion in the church and make them feel special. It was then much easier to go on and have a helpful discussion about baptism, without throwing all the theology in their face from the moment they knocked on the door.

For some, the service of Thanksgiving was actually all that they wanted and they decided not to go immediately on to baptism. They usually went away very appreciative of the service and became a warm 'fringe contact' to be kept in touch with and followed up as appropriate.

For those who did decide they wanted to go on to baptism, again there was the appreciative response to the Thanksgiving and therefore often a greater openness to engage with some proper preparation for the baptism. (Parents were often encouraged, as a sign of their wanting to take the baptism and its meaning seriously, to go on an Alpha course themselves). My own view, and I think that of the incumbent, was that the determination to come back for baptism and receive some sort of preparation, was in itself enough to proceed happily with the baptism. The Thanksgiving service was helpful pastorally, helpful liturgically as the 'rite' the parents felt they had a need for and helpful in allowing time for theological issues to be considered, as well as relationships built.

The church described in Family Snaps 1 at the beginning of the booklet is one with a very clear policy about using the Thanksgiving service and involving as many people as possible in the congregation, both in preparing for the service, taking part (some are invited to tell their own Christian story or to be interviewed about how their faith relates to their family life) and also in inviting people to come. It is seen as part of the task of all members of the church, and a leaflet is given to church members, to reinforce this, with the colourful slogan 'You can't leave the Vicar holding this baby!'

How to Make the Most of Thanksgiving Services

1. Make yourself familiar with the materials and the aim. Talk to one of the young families team if you want to discuss how you can get involved. With this leaflet you should find:

- The leaflet designed for parents. It gives simple answers to questions people might ask like 'Who is the service for?', 'What is the difference between this and christening?' and 'What will it be like?'
- A copy of the service card you can show to people if you want to.
- An invitation card.

2. Develop your baby-spotting abilities. For instance:

- If you are a young parent yourself, babies may come visiting you at home with their parents, or bump into you at the clinic or the Under Ones' club. You will be talking babies with other parents, and have plenty of opportunities to suggest they come along with you.
- Around the town: next time you are admiring a local baby pluck up courage to mention the next service. Have a leaflet handy, so people can go on thinking about it when you part. Do not pressurize—it is simply something we are offering to those who want an opportunity to thank God for their new baby.
- Use your imagination—and memory! What new babies have you heard about recently? Does that friend at work—the one who is sure he will have a son any day now—live near here? What about that girl who drifted away from church who's living on her own and about to have a baby? Or that new couple down the road? It is quite normal to get enthusiastic about babies, so join in the enthusiasm.
- Imagine what some of these conversations might be like, or try practising them on other members of your home group. For instance, a neighbour in your road has had a new baby, and you occasionally stop and chat in the street, you are congratulating her on the new arrival. 'Hi, Mary—how're you doing? And how's Lauren? Is she sleeping better

now?...I wonder whether you've thought of coming to one of our Thanksgiving services? A lot of people feel they need to say thank you to someone when they have a new baby, and our new service is meant for that. It does not mean you have got to come to church forever after! And it does not mean that you are saying that you know you are a Christian. It is just an opportunity for parents and families and friends to come and say thank you to God. I went to one a couple of months ago, when Jane's family were there with their new baby. It is a very lively sort of service, not the sort of thing you might expect from the church! And they give you a copy of one of the Gospels with the baby's name inside...'

Some weeks later Mary tackles you about wanting her baby done properly.

'I mean, that service we went to was not really a Christening—the vicar did not give the baby his name or pour water over him. How do we go about getting him christened?'

Do you know the answer? It is there in the leaflet we give out to parents who come enquiring about Baptism or Christening.

3. Pray—for the service and the opportunities it gives. Even if you are not bringing someone with you, it might be an idea to come to a Thanksgiving service so that you can speak from first-hand knowledge when you are inviting someone to come. And you can pray better when you can see what you are praying for!

Leaflet and Invitation Card

The leaflet this church has designed for parents is very personalized, with pictures of the church, of a Thanksgiving service in progress, and of the baby of one of the church members. It is set out in question and answer form, with questions like 'What is this service for?', 'What will happen at it?', 'What should the baby wear?' and 'How does christening fit in?'

The invitation card contains blank lines for church members to fill in the date of the next Thanksgiving service and the names of the children and parents, and states clearly what kind of event people are invited to. There is a tear-off reply portion which can be sent back in the post if necessary, with the parents' names and address, and the child's names.

Service Card

The church has its own abbreviated service card, suitable for use both on Sunday afternoons and when the service is fitted into a Sunday morning service. It looks something like the layout over the page, but with pictures of the church and service which tie it in with the explanatory leaflet. The Pastoral Introduction is printed in full.

Thanksgiving for the Gift of a Child at St ...

Introduction
- Welcome
- Hymn
- Introduction and prayer

Readings and Sermon

Thanksgiving and Blessing

Supporting friends may stand with the parents at the thanksgiving. One of them may present the children to the minister, and informal words may be said.

The minister says

> Do you receive *these children* as a gift from God?
> **We do.**
>
> Do you wish to give thanks to God and seek his blessing?
> **We do.**

The minister prays the prayer 'God our creator' which ends
> We praise you, Father, Son and Holy Spirit.
> **Blessed be God for ever.**

The minister says for each child
> What name have you given this child?

A parent or supporting friend replies
> *His/her* name is N.

The minister then takes the child and says the prayer of blessing. All join in the ending of the prayer:
> **May *they* learn to love all that is true,**
> **grow in wisdom and strength**
> **and, in due time, come through faith and baptism**
> **to the fullness of your grace;**
> **through Jesus Christ, our Lord.**
> **Amen.**

The minister prays for the parents

Giving of the Gospel

A copy of a Gospel is presented, with these words
Receive this book.
It is the good news of God's love.
Take it as your guide.

The minister may ask the supporting friends
Will you do all that you can to help and support *N and N* in the bringing up of *N*?
With the help of God, we will.

The minister may ask the wider family and friends
Will you do all that you can to help and support *this family*?
With the help of God, we will.

Prayers

This prayer may be said by the parents or by the whole congregation

God our creator,
we thank you for the gift of *these children*,
entrusted to our care.
May we be patient and understanding,
ready to guide and to forgive,
so that through our love
they may come to know your love;
through Jesus Christ our Lord.
Amen.

Additional prayers, ending with the Lord's Prayer.

Jesus taught us to call God our Father,
and so in faith and trust we say

Our Father in heaven...

This service card is produced cheaply, in sufficient quantities for copies to be given to those who enquire or attend.

Conclusion

It should be possible to multiply stories and examples like these, and to encourage people to share their experience of this service. Here we have a useful tool for a variety of occasions and purposes, which God can use in drawing people to himself, moving them on towards baptism, affirming both children and families.